Green Tea

&

Other Forms of Meditation

Healing Benefits for Life's Bruises

Latrea Wyche

Copyright

Printed in the United States of America

First Printing, 2015
2nd Edition, 2017

ISBN-13: 978-1-942022-98-5
ISBN10: 192022980

the **Butterfly Typeface**

The Butterfly Typeface Publishing
PO BOX 56193
Little Rock Arkansas 72215

Healing Benefits For Life's Bruises

Latrea Wyche

Green Tea &
Other Forms of Meditation

Other books by

Latrea Wyche

Bruised But Not Broken:
The Workbook Series

Overcoming the Emotional
Barriers of Disability

Your Next Level!

The Purpose Driven You!

Green Tea is a combination of my personal life experiences that I pray will help you grow in your life.

Healing Benefits for Life ...

DEDICATION

This book is dedicated to anyone who knows that despite what they were *told* or made to *believe*, they were created to be someone special.

'Learn to discover your healing from within.'

FOREWORD

Each and every person is given a purpose in his/her life. For some, finding their purpose in life might be easy. For the vast majority of us, it can be hard. However, as hard as it may be for you to find your purpose understand that it is there.

It is often believed that there no one is on this earth who is not supposed to make an impact. Your purpose is how you will make an impact in this world. Discover it! Embrace it! No matter what hardship you have endured to this point or might endure in the future, those hardships are not only meant to make you stronger but to show others how it IS POSITIVE to overcome and to grow from those experiences.

If you are reading this book, you are in a truly unique position. Individuals with disabilities are often viewed as not being able to make a great contribution to society or as lacking the ability to make an impact in our world. We all know this to be untrue.

By reading this book, you are taking a step in finding your purpose and finding what it is that you have to offer the world and those around you. You have the unique opportunity to show the world that a disability will NOT stop you in the different areas of your life. You can be a voice and a role model for those that will surely come after you. As you read this book, build your courage, strength, and determination! You are an asset that the world is in desperate need of...

Are you ready?

ACKNOWLEDGMENTS

First and foremost, I would like to thank God for allowing me to be a voice for the voiceless. I would also like to thank Him for His patience, His grace, His mercy, and for loving me when I did not love myself. Secondly, I would like to thank my husband, Barry Wyche Jr., and my daughter, Olivia, for their love and support and for just allowing me to be me. Words cannot express how much I love you guys.

Next, I would like thank my mothers, Donna Mance and Shirley Kenney. Most people consider themselves fortunate to have one; I however, am fortunate enough to have two.

These are two of the most remarkable women I know. I have seen them struggle just to hold it together, and because of them, I have learned so much about how to be a wife, a mother, and woman. They will never know how grateful I am that God chose me to be their daughter.

Special thanks to my spiritual parents, Pastor Frederick and Rashida Potts, for believing in me when no one else did and for helping me find the voice I never knew I had.

I would also like to thank two of my biggest cheerleaders (outside my family), Jerval Johnson and Garlinda Price. Those two women have been in my corner from day one always pushing me to be great. They saw the greatness in me when I did not see it. When I wanted to throw in the towel, they were there to throw it right back at me.

Thanks to all of WOP (Breath of God Women of Prosperity). I love each one of you ladies. You all have brought something special to my life.

This next woman I want to thank ... I really don't know what to say. 'Miss Iris,' as I like to call her, I want to thank you, 'Miss Iris,' for just giving me a platform to allow my voice to be heard.

Last, but not least, I want to thank a special group of people-my haters. I don't have to name you specifically because you know who you are.

You said I would not be anything. You shut the door in my face and would not give me a chance. You took one look at me and wrote me off because I did not look like everyone else. I thank you because had you not written me off, I would have never gained the added strength needed to make my dreams a reality.

Table of Contents

Who Are You?

Who are you?
When the lights go out
Who are you?
When the curtain close and
everyone goes home
Who are you?
When you remove the mask
Who are you?
When you are in your alone space
When there is no one staring back
in the mirror at you
When you look at yourself
what do you see?
A shell of remains
of what used to be
Or the reflection of the person
you wish you could be?

So many times we get caught up in the hustle and bustle of life that we forget who we are within ourselves. As women of faith, we wear so many hats, at least I know I do. I am a wife, mother, sister, aunt, Sunday school teacher, Elder, author, and Life Coach.

However, in wearing these hats, we must realize that none of them are who we really are. They are just roles we play depending on the situation.

Never allow your role in life to cause you to lose track of who you really are. Who you really are is the person left behind when the lights go out, and you are alone. Who you are is the person standing in front of the mirror after you have removed the mask of whatever role you're playing.

When you are staring in the face of fear because you have *lost the person you used be; the person staring back at you.*

Green Tea & Other Forms of Meditation by Latrea Wyche

First Sip

--Green Tea--

The Side Effects of Bruises

Someone famous once said, "Two of the greatest days of your life are the day you were born and the day you understand why." The understanding why part can sometimes be the most difficult part, at least it was for me.

I felt like I was stumbling around in a dark room looking for the light switch. Deep down inside, I always knew I was here for a special reason. After all of the things I have been through to get to this point, I better be here for a special reason.

I did all the things a person was supposed to do; I went to college, earned a degree, got married, had a child, when back to college for a second degree, and worked here and there, but I still felt like something was missing. I still felt out of place.

See, people tend to be under the misconception that once you have achieved what the worlds deems to be success then whatever issues you're dealing with are going to magically disappear - that is so far form the truth. If you did not love yourself before the degree, trust me no piece of paper can replace self-love. I want to make one important point here: no matter how many accomplishments you have hanging on your wall, if you don't love yourself none of that matters.

It was not until I went back to college for the third time that the Lord stopped me and said, "It's time for you to take your rightful place." Now, I had no idea what He meant, but I know this had to have been Him because when I tried to return to school, I failed almost every class and ended up getting kicked out of school.

When God wants to move you, He will oftentimes make places and situations so uncomfortable it will seem like every door is being closed or blocked and you have no choice but to go in the direction He is trying to send you in, and in most cases the direction will lead you right to your purpose.

Besides, what if you lived your entire life without ever fulfilling your God given purpose? Think of how empty the world would be without your mark.

Long story short, I ended up becoming a licensed professional life coach and started a business called *Discovering Your Abilities*.

Discovering Your Abilities (DYA) is a life coaching company that was developed with the sole purpose of empowering and providing a platform for people with various disabilities to discover who they are outside of their disabilities. DYA is a client centered company that is focused on helping clients find their voice, their talents, skill sets, and provides them with tools to help them draw on their internal strengths.

I want this book to empower you and give you another perspective other than what you may have seen or been told. After reading this book, I want you to understand that despite what you have been through or what you are currently going through, you can make it to the other side of the pain.

So many times, we get caught up on our *right now*, not understanding and our *right now* is a temporary situation.

The journey may not be easy, but if you continue to hold on to the seed of faith that has been placed in you from conception, you will make it. You will be everything that you are determined to be. Notice that I said what YOU are determined to be.

This means that at some point in your life, you are going to have to decide that you are going to be the best YOU that you know how to be, and with that, you can achieve whatever you put your mind to do. There are healing benefits to your bruised life!

Breakthrough

--Green Tea--

The Storm Is Over

Is your storm the problem or is your storm just a symptom of a deeper issue that you have tried to suppress? Interesting question huh? It's something to really sit back and ponder.

So many times, we find ourselves in the midst of a storm or a state of confusion and we are so fixed on the storm itself (the right now) that we forget there is life after the storm. "Oh, this is so hard," or "How am I ever going to get out of this?" How about my personal favorite, "Why does this have to happen to me?"

Through all the whining, (Yes, I said it … whining.) we fail to look at the big picture. Well, there are actually two pictures here:

One - How did you end up in this particular situation? If this is not the first time you have found yourself in this place, how you did end up back here?

Two - What could you have done differently that would have prevented you from ending up in a situation that (A) is bad or that (B) in which you don't want to be.

Let's explore this for a second. If this is a place that you have found yourself in for the 2nd or 3rd time, then it's probably time to really start examining the life choices that are causing you to be in the situation.

Why is taking responsibility so hard for us? I say us because I have often had issues with this as well. We find ourselves in the midst of an unpleasant situation, and the first thing we want to do is blame someone else. "If my momma had not done this, I wouldn't be in this situation," or "If my daddy hadn't left me, I would not be like this." Some of that may be true to a certain extent, but when you become a certain age it's time to stop *placing* the blame and start *taking* the blame for the overall outcome of your life. I mean, really, at what age do your parents or lack thereof stop being the reason for your reckless lifestyle? I am serious! At what age do you stop using people as an excuse for why *you* are not doing what *you* were created to do?

Something I have had to learn in life is our parents can only give us what they have to give, so if they don't have it, they can't give it. If they were never given any love, they are not going to know how to love. If they were never shown compassion, they won't know how to show compassion.

This was something that I had to learn about my own mother. She never knew how to properly show love because as a kid, she was never properly shown love. I used to always say, "...she lived her life on a rollercoaster and me and my sister were just along for the ride." And I still believe that, but as an adult I now understand why.

The flip side to this (Yes, there is a flip side!) is that there are experiences which take place in our past that send us certain messages about who we are and what we are capable of accomplishing.

Depending on whether these experiences are positive or negative will determine the message that is received.

For example, suppose as a child you wanted to be a doctor, but no one in your family is a doctor. Every time you talked about wanting to be a doctor, someone told you it is not going happen because there has never been a doctor in the family before. What if you are told that you need to stop talking such foolishness.

Studies have shown that if you tell someone the same *thing* over long periods of time, beginning in their childhood, and that *thing* is all they are exposed to from the people around them, that *thing* is what they start to believe. In most cases the *thing* is a negative *thing* and not true, but it now becomes their only frame of reference.

That child grows up believing that no matter how hard they try they will never be a doctor. They stop trying not only to fulfill their dream of being a doctor, but they stop trying period.

This behavior carries on into adulthood. There are certain habits that we have now that resulted from an experience in our past.

For example, have you ever met someone who just seems mean all the time? Someone who is just mean for no reason. Someone who never smiles, is never happy, and as a matter of fact, you hate to see her or him coming because the individual is like a dark cloud.

I promise you they were not always like that. Somewhere in their past, (likely in their childhood) someone hurt them or sent them a negative message about themselves, so they now refuse to allow anyone to get too close for fear of rejection or hurt. They use being mean as a defense shield.

So what does all this have to do with a storm: storms are created by the negative messages we were sent.

The next time you find yourself in the midst of a storm or state of confusion, I urge you to do some soul searching. Where could this storm have come from? Is it a symptom of a bigger problem that you don't want to pay attention to or is it something new that has developed?

Once you are able to find the root of your storm or confusion, the more likely you are to prevent it from returning.

Ready

--Green Tea--

You're Not Ready

You're not ready to be with me.

You're not ready to be who I need you to be.

You're not ready to sacrifice.

You're not ready to let me in your life.

So, tell me how long must I wait.

Fore I hear you tell me

that you want me to stay.

Cause I can't hold on

to what I can't see.

So, love me or set me free.

This poem is a perfect example of how the mind can conspire with the heart to play tricks on the mind.

The poem, *You're Not Ready*, came out of a relationship that I was in almost fifteen years ago. I am not going to say that I was in love per se, but I was in love with the potential of what could have been. I became so caught up in the potential that I missed who the person really was. This poem is a perfect example of how the mind can conspire with the heart to play tricks on the mind.

Rule of thumb: Don't ever get so caught up in what someone has the potential to be that you miss the more important things like who they really are.

At the end of the day, who he really was wasn't what I needed at the time, and as hard as it was, I had to walk away.

I replayed the breakup in my mind over and over again. Each time I told myself that I was going to end it only to end up talking myself out of it and making all types of excuses as to why I should stay when I was not really happy.

As I write this now, it sounds so crazy - why would I stay in a situation that I knew I was not happy with. I had hope that at some point the situation would change and that the change will not happen. Like so many women, we think we can change him into what we need him to be.

In my mind, I knew leaving was the right thing to do, but my heart was a whole other story.

I remember thinking to myself, "I am going to be alone again? I have to start all over again." I wondered, "Is all that worth being happy?" The answer was yes.

Our last encounter seems like it was only yesterday.

I was in college at the time, and he came to visit me on campus. He ended up staying the night, As I lay in bed next to him, I remember thinking, "I can't continue doing this. This is not fair to me." I decided then and there that this would be the last time I would see him.

The next morning, we got up, we walked to his car, and he drove me back to the front of my dorm. It was the worst kind of quiet during a very short ride. It was almost like we both knew it was the end, but neither one of us wanted to admit it. I guess that's why when I started talking he didn't interrupt me.

We both got out the car. He walked me to the door, and we said our goodbyes for the last time. I remember thinking, "*You're not ready.*"

useable

--Green Tea--

Prepare to Serve

I had a conversation with a good friend not too long ago. She and her husband were told by their pastor that they would soon begin the process to become Deacons at their church. She was telling me how scared she was which is normal under all accounts. But the one thing that stuck out to me the most was when she said she felt like she was not ready because there were some things that she needed to clean up before she could answer the call God had placed on her life.

This is not the first time I have heard or experienced this. I actually felt this way when I was going through the process to be an Elder. I thought I had to get clean before God could use me.

So many of you are also under this *crazy* assumption. You feel that in order for you to answer the call God has placed on your life, you must be perfect or very close to it.

Ok, there are a couple of things wrong with that theory:

One - No one is perfect and believe it or not, God knows that we are not perfect. He does not expect us to be.

Two - God knew us before we knew ourselves. Therefore, He knew every mistake we were going to ever make. It is because of His love, mercy, and grace that He continues to love us in spite of our sins.

Our sins and shortcomings do not erase the call that God has placed on our lives. Sometimes they might delay the process, but they will never diminish it.

Three - If we could clean up our own mess don't you think we would have done so by now?

Throughout the Bible, you will find countless stories where God used what some would consider outcasts to carry out His plan.

One story that comes to mind is Samson. If you have read the story of Samson, you know he was a physical tower of strength. He was a people's champ because of his physical strength. But if you read further, you will discover that he was not used by God until he was at his weakest point physically. Crazy huh? God will do that to us sometimes.

Another example is the story of Moses. Moses had a speech impairment, yet he was used to deliver the people of Israel. The funny thing about this example is that Moses went to God (as we often do) and told Him that he could not be used because of his speech impairment and that the people would not listen to him.

We do the same thing. We go to God with a bunch of *excuses* as to why we can't walk in our calling. That's funny to me because we go to God like He doesn't know what we have going on. I mean after all He did create us, so of course He would know what ailments we may have.

God will never give us a task that He knows we can't complete. What I am basically saying is when God decides He wants to use you, you have to have faith that He has made the right decision and allow Him to do the rest.

Increase

--Green Tea--

I Rise

I rise from the ashes
from my brokenness.
I break free from the chains
that hold my dreams captive.
I remove the layers of my past.
I strip away the scars of my pain.
I rise to take my rightful place,
A place that was once
so distant to me.
As I pull off layer by layer,
I slowly began to see
The woman I was born to be
That God created in me.
The person people never took
the time to see.
I hear the voices calling out to me.
Come forth.
Come forth;
take your rightful place
It is your time to rise!

Like many of my poems, I have no idea where 'I Rise' came from. I was riding in the car on my way to the airport to speak at an anti-bullying rally. I opened my journal and started writing; this is what came out.

The crazy part about that experience is that I have not felt the same since writing this poem.

I could feel the layers of shame falling off with each word I wrote. The years of guilt and not understanding my purpose were being washed away with each line.

I guess you can say this is the one that changed my life. *I truly began to rise ...*

Significance

--Green Tea--

Empty Spaces

This meditation came about after speaking to a young man whose self-esteem was in the toilet low. I mean lower than I had ever seen, especially for a man. Admittedly, he did have some psychosocial challenges that made his life somewhat difficult at times. Despite that, I knew deep down inside he was a good kid that could accomplish great things with his life. But before that could happen, he had to believe that it was possible.

He would often tell me, "I am only living for my girlfriend. She is what is keeping me alive." Now at first I thought, "Ok, he must just really be in love." But as time went on, I saw it was much deeper than that - at least to him it was.

I would try to convince him that he was a wonderful person outside of his girlfriend, but for whatever reason, he just could not see it. He had put so much of himself into her that he could not see himself existing without her. It sounds crazy doesn't it? Well, believe it or not we do it all the time.

This happens when we don't understand or realize our self-worth. For people with disabilities (or those who have been in abusive relationships), we get to a place where we are just happy to have someone in our lives. So, we allow (or become convinced) that our lives would be nothing without them.

We put so much of ourselves in another person that we forget our own value outside of that person. This I call it *putting all of your eggs in someone else's basket.*

Many times, we look to other people to fill up our empty spaces. We want them to add value to our existence and to somehow make life meaningful for us.

When people we choose for this *difficult* task don't measure up or somehow don't meet our expectations, two things tend to happen.

One - We walk away from the situation feeling empty and lost.

Two - We want to blame *them* for not being what we need them to be for us.

We must learn to validate ourselves for who we are as individuals and not *solely* on our capabilities or our flaws. Many times, we want to omit our flaws, but understand this, our flaws are what make us who we are just as much as our capabilities.

Enough

--Green Tea--

More than Enough

I grew up in a household where my needs were not always the top concern. My parents had their own issues. My dad was an alcoholic, and my mom abused crack. This made life very difficult for me.

Along with all of the drama at home, I was born with a rare genetic disorder called Pfeiffer Syndrome. Pfeiffer Syndrome is a genetic disorder that causes the bones in your skull and other parts of your body to not fuse properly. Because of my disability, I had some facial differences which caused me to look different than most kids. I am also visually and hearing impaired. Throughout my life, I have had 30-45 operations.

I would go to school and get teased on a daily basis about something that I had no control over. Then, I would come home to find there was no food because my parents used the money to purchase drugs and alcohol. Due to my home life, I would often go to school in dirty clothes and would be hungry which only added fuel to the fire.

It was during fifth grade; I think that a big camping trip was coming up. This was a big deal for the fifth grade, and for most of us, this was our first time really sleeping away from home. I was so excited; it was all I could talk about although it was only for two nights. It was a big deal for me!

I brought the permission slip home, had my mom sign it, and returned it the next day. I just knew I was going.

About a week before the trip, I started getting things together. I chose the bag I wanted to use to pack my clothes and made sure I had everything I needed: a toothbrush, toothpaste and soap. Still, there was something missing - clothes. I told my mom that I needed her to wash clothes, so I would have clean clothes to take with me. I reminded her every day that week. Finally, the day before the trip came and still no clean clothes. I decided to take matters into my own hands. I put all my clothes in the bath tub to wash them. I don't even remember what soap I used. After I "washed" my clothes, I hung them on the porch to dry. I just knew they would be dry the next morning. The next morning, I got up and realized the clothes were just as wet as they were the night before. However, no one was going to stop me from going on the trip, so I balled up all my wet clothes in a bag and went to school.

When I got to school, the teachers were loading everyone's bags onto the bus. When a teacher picked up my bag, she noticed it was a lot heavier than the other bags. She decided to look inside, and that's when she discovered the wet clothes. I told her the story of how I tried to wash the clothes myself. She decided to pack up all the clothes and took them to be washed and dried.

By the age of twelve, my home life became very toxic, so much so that my sister and I were placed in foster care. I remained there until age sixteen when I was adopted.

My years in foster care were the roughest years of my life: being bounced from home to home, not knowing where I was going to end up, and trying to find a place to fit in.

I remember one home in particular. I remember every foster home I have ever been in, but this one really stands out to me probably because this was the one where I was treated the worse.

My foster mother was a single parent with two girls, a baby and a teenager. This woman could not stand the sight of me. Because I was disabled, I was made to stay in my room. I was not allowed to sit in the living room with everyone else. I had to eat from paper plates, use plastic forks, spoons and cups - things that could be thrown away.

I remember one time we all went to the mall together, but my sister and I were not allowed to go into the mall with the foster mother because she did not want to be seen with me. So, we sat in that hot car for what felt like forever.

Each one of our life experiences sends us messages about ourselves and the world around us. Whether the message is good or bad is determined upon whether the experience was good or bad. In this case I received the message that I was not enough. No matter how good I was behaving or how good my grades where I would never be enough.

Eventually, I was adopted into a family that loved me as much as they could, considering we were not biologically related. Inside I was not really sure how I felt about the whole situation. I mean, I knew that I would be safe, and it was probably the best situation for me and my sister, but all I really wanted was for my mother to climb in the bed with me (like she did when I was little), wrap her arms around me, hug all my pain and fears away, and tell me that no matter what she loved me and everything was going to be alright. Needless to say, that never happened.

As the years went on and I became an adult, it was like that little girl was somehow still trapped inside of me, and all she yearned for was for her mother to come rescue her.

I remember constantly questioning God. "Why am I not enough for my mother to stop using drugs?" "Why was I not enough for her to want to take care of us?" I replayed those questions over and over in my mind trying to understand why things worked out the way they did. I was trying to uncover some hidden mystery that no one could seem to solve.

That was until one day, in the midst of my seeking, I heard the voice of the Lord say, "You ask why I am not enough. You constantly seek the approval of other people, but you never work that hard to seek My approval." The Lord went on to ask, "Why am *I* not enough? I have brought you through every foster home situation, every operation, and every low peak in your life, but that's still not enough for you."

From that day forth, I made a conscience decision that as long as I have God, I will have more than enough!

Have you ever felt that you were not enough or that you had to be more than what you were in order to be accepted?

steadfast

--Green Tea--

Still

I am still here.

> You thought you killed me with your words,

But I am still here.

> You thought you would destroy me

>> with your lies of forever,

But I am still here.

> You thought you would break my spirit

as you have so many times before,

> But to your surprise,

>> I am still here.

The day you walked out

> was supposed to have been my end,

>> But I am still here.

Each brick you have thrown at me

> should have broken me into pieces.

>> But instead I used those bricks

>>> as symbols of my inner strength

The inner-strength you worked so hard to rob me of

> But guess what..........

>> I am still here!

'Still' is one of those poems that just *jumped* into my spirit. I don't know where it came from or why it was given to me. When I think about it, it is a testament to people everywhere who have ever been repeatedly knocked down and left for dead.

I am *still* here. No matter how hard you try to break me, I am *still* here.

The poem is indicative of how resilient the human spirit is. It will not die.

Last Sip

--Green Tea--

That Which Holds Us

We are such hoarders. We hold on to everything: furniture, clothes, experiences, and even feelings ... Hmmmm interesting concept.

How does one hoard feelings and experiences?

That was an interesting concept for me understand. Why do we hold on to things that happened twenty or thirty years ago? These things that often times keep us *stuck* in the feelings and the emotions that the situation created.

What people fail to see is that when we (and I say we because I am guilty of this as well) hold on to old stuff, there is no room for any of the new things with which God wants to bless us. He can't bless us with anything new because we refuse to let go of the old stuff that keeps us stuck.

Have you ever found yourself stuck in a situation because you were holding on to that experience?

The big question remains. Why do we hold on to things, especially experiences that hurt us? Well, there are two reasons for this:

One - It feels comfortable. Sometimes we can carry something for so long it becomes part of who we are. The same can be said about feelings. You can carry hurt and anger around for so long that they become a part of your personality.

For example, I knew a woman that would hold on to certain feelings for what would seem like forever. If someone said or did something that she thought was hurtful, she would hold on to that bad experience for years. Every time she saw the person, that hurt she felt would show up. The crazy thing about this is that the person who hurt her had forgotten about the situation and simply moved on while she was still holding on to the hurt and the anger. So, she was left stuck in the situation.

Two - It gives them someone to blame. Many times, we encounter experiences that might not be our fault. Someone might have intentionally hurt us or allowed someone else to hurt us.

At what point do you let the feelings of hurt and anger go? When do you decide that you are no longer going to allow this feeling to control you?

Hurt and anger are a dangerous combination and a very dangerous state of mind in which to dwell. There are people sitting in jail right now who will never see the light of day all because they could not let hurt and anger go.

Don't let the bruises of life hold you captive. There is healing in your bruises if you will reach out to God for help. If you are not careful, you can build a whole community centered around what someone said or did you to over 10-15 years ago.

Silence

As I sit in the silence,

I hear the whispers of my pain.

As they call out my name,

Why do you hurt yourself in vain?

What is this pain I feel I can't
explain?

As the night falls

And darkness covers the sky,

I run and hide from the terrors of the
unknown.

The fears I keep locked inside my
soul

I don't understand.

I can't make sense of it.

Until then I sit

in the silence of my pain.

I was actually advised to not include the poem "Silence" in this book because it is kind of *dark*, while the rest of the book is so *uplifting* and *encouraging.*

However, the truth of the matter is that there are times in life where we are going to have dark moments. We are going to have moments where we aren't going to know if we can make it or not.

Whether we want to accept it or not, dark moments are a part of life. The dark days are when the test truly comes.

Everyone can laugh and smile when everything is going right for them, but can you still laugh and smile while everything around you is falling down?

Can you still smile while your heart breaks with each beat? Yes, you can because dark moments do not last forever. At some point the sun is going to shine again. At some point the rain will stop, the clouds will move, and you will no longer find yourself within the *silence* of your pain.

About The Author

Latrea Wyche is 38 years old, originally from PG County MD, and is a Disabilities Empowerment coach, a motivational speaker and a published author. She currently resides in Fayetteville NC with her eleven-year-old daughter.

Born with Phiffer Syndrome, a rare genetic disorder that causes the bones in the skull and other parts of the body to not fuse properly, Latrea has vision and hearing impairment and has endured more than 30-45 operations to correct various health problems.

Dealing with major family issues, including drug addicted parents, she and her sister entered the foster care system when Latrea was twelve and her sister was four. This is where they would remain until Latrea reached the age of sixteen when she and her sister would be adopted.

Throughout their time in the foster care system both girls encountered countless abuse. Latrea being the oldest, always felt It was her job to take care of her sister, something she has been doing since her sister was born. She felt to need to make sure her sister was taken care of, even sometimes at the sacrifice of herself.

Through it all Latrea has managed to defy the odds; earning a BA in Psychology, a Master's in Education. Latrea became a Professional Certified Life Coach, as well as certified in disabilities ministries leadership. Latrea has also had her book "Intimate Conversations with God" featured as a special book at the 2017 NAACP convention. Latrea also travels all over the state of North Carolina speaking at various disability organizations.

"As a Disabilities Empowerment coach, it is my goal to empower, motivate, and encourage the disabled population to live above the limits of society, by providing a voice that teaches them to speak their personal truth."

Facebook: www.facebook.com/coachLatrea

Twitter: https://twitter.com/coachlatrea

Email: coachlatreawyche@gmail.com

Instagram: https://www.instagram.com/coachlatrea79/

YouTube:
https://www.youtube.com/channel/UCFLWR0q1XDY9zjwgeThfrlg

The Butterfly Typeface Publishing

"We make good GREAT!"

Iris M Williams – Owner

The Butterfly Typeface

PO Box 56193

Little Rock Arkansas

501.823.0574

www.thebutterflytypeface.com

info@butterflytypeface.com